HELP ME
LEVEL UP
A Growth Mindset Manual for Finding
Purpose & Power
Afolake Agunbiade

Published by: CADsync Consults
www.cadsyncconsults.com
Folake.agunbiade@cadsyncconsults.com

Revised Edition (2025)

National Library of Nigeria Cataloguing-In-Publication Data:

- Name: Afolake Agunbiade
- Title: Help Me Level Up!
- Category: Self Help
- ISBN: 978-978-696-168-2

Cover design by BlazeyWorks -
blazeyworks@gmail.com

Printed in the Federal Republic of Nigeria
by CADsync Consults

Table Of Content

DEDICATION

To every child who was told they weren't enough
To every teenager searching for meaning and clarity
To every adult still healing from what they didn't receive…This book is for you.
May you always remember:
Your past is not your prison.
Your mistakes are not your identity.
And your future is still unfolding with purpose, with power, and with grace.
You were born to grow.
You were made for more.
And the world is better with your light in it.

ACKNOWLEDGMENTS

This book was born out of countless casual and therapy conversations, courageous stories, and silent breakthroughs I've witnessed in my work with children, teenagers, and adults. I am deeply grateful to every young person who ever dared to be honest with me, every parent who trusted me with their child's or teenager's heart, and every reader who chooses to grow even when it's hard and heart-breaking.

To my family (Dr. Oluwaseye, Lana, Nimi, Imisi, Isimi Agunbiade) you are my first classroom in love, resilience, grit and faith. Thank you for your patience, support and unwavering belief in the work I do.

To my mentors and numerous mentees, thank you for helping me stretch, reflect, and rise. Your impact lives in the pages of this book.

To my team at CADsync Consults (Israel Ojuade, Gideon Alejo, Stella Chiedu & Co), and to my professional community, thank you for pushing the boundaries of what it means to care, to serve, and to lead.

And finally, to you, my dearest reader, thank you for trusting me to walk alongside you on this journey. I pray these words stir something brave in your soul and leave you better than they found you.

Cheers to a life of meaning, growth, and purpose.

FOREWORD

We are all born with the same invisible tool which is a mind full of possibility; however, somewhere between growing up and growing old, many of us begin to believe a lie that our abilities are fixed, our purpose is blurry, and our story is stuck.

As a psychologist who has walked beside hundreds of children, teenagers, and families, I have seen first-hand what happens when we swap shame for self-belief, fear for curiosity, and perfection for progress. **That shift, however small, is what we call a growth mindset.**

This book was born out of my deep desire to help people of all ages understand that growth is not just a school subject or corporate buzzword. It is a way of living, thinking, loving, and leading. And more importantly, it is the foundation for discovering one's true purpose.

Whether you are reading this as a parent, student, teacher, coach, or simply a person who wants more out of life, you are welcome here. This book is not a textbook.
It is a companion.
A guide.
A mirror.

It is a soft but firm voice that says you don't have to have it all figured out to move forward. You just need to believe that you can grow."

So, read it slowly. Reflect often and return to it whenever life feels uncertain because your purpose is not somewhere far off in the future; it's hidden in your mindset, waiting to be uncovered.

Welcome to your next chapter loaded with hope and conviction!

Afolake Agunbiade
Psychologist | Purpose Advocate | Growth Companion | Acceleration Coach

FOREWORD II

We all arrive at a moment in life where we begin to ask deeper questions: Why am I here? What is the meaning of this season? Is there more to me than what I've known or settled for?

This book does not just answer those questions it, awakens something eternal inside of you.

There are books that inspire, and then there are books that activate and accelerate : Help Me Level Up is the latter.

In a world where many feel stuck between potential and purpose, where fear and self-doubt cloud our paths, my dear friend and sister, Folake Agunbiade, has given us more than a book, she has given us a gift. With the wisdom of a seasoned psychologist and the compassion of someone who deeply understands the journey of transformation, she has created a roadmap for rising from within.

This book speaks to the heart of what it means to grow on purpose. It gently challenges limiting beliefs, invites the reader into radical self-awareness, and equips us with tools to unlock a powerful, growth-centered mindset. What I love most is how it makes the complex simple and the distant achievable. Whether you're struggling to start, afraid to pivot, or hungry for more, this book will meet you at whatever point you are and water your roots and stir your potential.

I have witnessed Folake's passion for people, her excellence in her field, and her unwavering commitment to helping others rise. She doesn't just teach growth, she lives it. Her words will remind you that your next level isn't a fantasy, it's a decision and is achievable.

As someone who has walked the path of radical transformation and walks and works with people through pain, transformation, and healing, I've learned that discovering purpose is not a grand arrival but a daily unfolding. And growth is not always loud or visible sometimes, it's simply the courage to take one more step, even when you're unsure.
Every page is an invitation to break out of survival, fear, and delay and to step fully into the life you were created to live.

Prepare to be stretched. Prepare to be seen. And most of all, prepare to remember who you were before the world told you to forget.

Tega Omogor
Substance Use Therapist | Inner Healing Advocate - Flourish Life Center | Speaker

ENDORSEMENT

There are moments in life when clarity arrives not with noise, but in a calm, persistent voice that speaks directly to your heart. For me, such voice came through the pages of Help Me Level Up by Folake Agunbiade.

Before encountering this transformative book, I found myself navigating life with a sense of motion but lacking direction. I was busy doing a lot, but not necessarily fulfilled.

Then I crossed paths with Folake Agunbiade, a woman whose insight, discipline, and leadership go far beyond titles. As the Lead Consultant at Cadsync Consults Limited, Folake Agunbiade posseses the ability to simplify the complex and ignite the hunger for purpose in others. Her mentorship style in words, example, and action, reshaped my understanding of growth, impact, and personal evolution.

"Help Me Level Up" didn't just speak to me; it challenged me. It gave answers to the questions of my heart.

This book is a gift. Let it challenge you, stretch you, and ofcourse, help you level up.

Victor Adoga
President, Blaznation Global

INTRODUCTION:

Why Mindset Matters in the Universal Search for Your Life Purpose

My journey to becoming is summed up beautifully in this quote, which you will hear me say so often if you have ever heard me speak or teach:

"A person is always in the process of becoming". The big question is: Into what?

Have you ever come across a child whose questions are endless, dreams are big, and experiments are fearless? Maybe you've encountered a teenager who struggles with identity, compares themselves to others, and wonders, "What am I really good at?"

Or hold on a minute; is that child or teenager you?
Maybe you've been that young adult, feeling stuck in a job that pays the bills but leaves your soul empty. Or an older person asking quietly, "Did my life really matter?"

What if I told you that the way you think about yourself is more powerful than any grade, job title, or even past mistake? Sounds simple. But it's true. Your mindset—the beliefs you hold about your abilities, your potential, and your worth is the lens through which you view the world.

And like any lens, it can either bring things into focus… or keep them blurry.

The actual truth is that at every age, we are all searching for meaning. This book is about two powerful forces that shape the search:

i. Your mindset and

ii. Your sense of purpose.

Whether you're a child or teenager still figuring it all out, a midlife adult seeking a reset, or a parent or mentor helping others grow, you'll find that what you believe about yourself and your capacity to grow matters more than you think.

Growth Mindset: A Key to Becoming

Psychologist Carol Dweck coined the term "Growth Mindset" to describe the belief that our abilities and intelligence can be developed through effort, learning, and resilience. In contrast, a fixed mindset assumes that talent, intelligence, and personality are static you either "have it" or you don't. Your mindset, often shaped in childhood, influences how you respond to challenges, interpret failure, and how willing you are to try again. Most importantly, it affects how you pursue purpose. Because the truth is: Finding purpose isn't a one-time discovery. It's a lifelong journey and a mindset that determines how far you'll go.

Purpose is a human need, not a luxury; so, it is not reserved for famous inventors, spiritual leaders, or influencers with perfect morning routines. Purpose is the quiet compass inside every one of us. It's what makes you feel alive, useful, and connected. Purpose also doesn't just "show up." It grows. Like a seed, it needs nurturing through curiosity, mistakes, learning, and reflection. That's where mindset and purpose meet: one shapes how you grow, the other shapes where you grow toward.

This book will help you:

i. Understand how your mindset was formed and how to change it

ii. Explore what "purpose" means across the stages of life

iii. Learn tools to grow through failure, doubt, and uncertainty

iv. Use your relationships, environment, and passions to shape a meaningful life

v. Help others—children, teens, friends, or family develop these same tools

I'm a psychologist who works with children and teenagers every day. But the truth is, I've seen the same questions and struggles in people of every age, viz,

“Am I enough?”

“What am I here for?”

“Can I really change?”

This book is written for you, whether you're a curious teenager, a struggling parent, a burned-out adult, or a wise elder who wants to reflect and give back. Each chapter contains examples and tools that speak across generations. You'll find stories of kids, teens, adults, and elders, because growth and purpose are not bound by age. “You don't need to have all the answers, But you do need to believe you can grow”.

CHAPTER 01

MINDSET 101 – WHAT YOU BELIEVE SHAPES WHO YOU BECOME

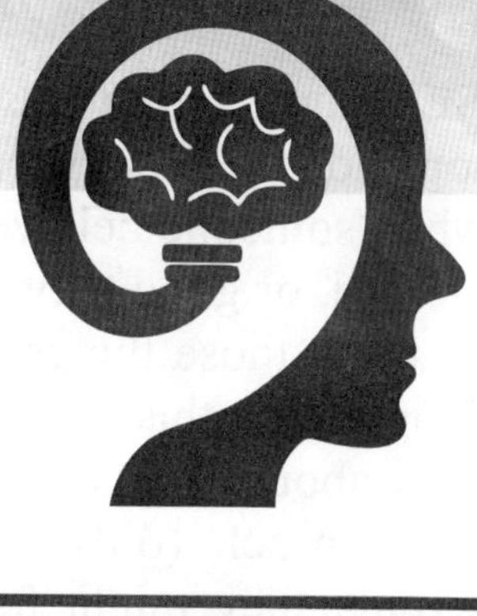

"Whether you think you can or you think you can't, you're right."

Henry Ford

Chapter 1:

MINDSET 101 – WHAT YOU BELIEVE SHAPES WHO YOU BECOME

What Is Mindset? Fixed vs Growth - The Invisible Divide

At its core, your mindset is the invisible lens through which you see the world and yourself. It's not just about how optimistic or pessimistic you are. It's about what you believe about your ability to change, grow, and improve. Let's start here: there are two basic types of mindsets—

i. Fixed and

ii. Growth.

A FIXED MINDSET says, "I'm either smart or I'm not. I either have talent or I don't. I either succeed or I fail." A fixed mindset is when someone believes that who they are, how smart, talented, or good they are at something can't change. They think those things are just the way they were born. People with this mindset often believe that success is mostly about talent (about 60%) and that effort doesn't matter much (only 40%). So, when something goes wrong, they might feel like it means they're not good enough or that they've failed as a person. Their thought pattern is: "If I'm not good at it now, I'll never be." That kind of thinking can make learning and growing much harder.

How do you know if you have a fixed mindset?

Here are some signs that someone might be stuck in this kind of thinking:

i. They avoid trying new things if they think they might mess up.

ii. They have a hard time bouncing back when something doesn't go their way.

iii. They try to hide their mistakes instead of learning from them.

iv. They often say things like, "I can't do this," or "I'm just not good at it.

In contrast, A GROWTH MINDSET says, "I can learn. I can change. I can improve, even if I'm not there yet." Now pause and ask yourself: WHICH VOICE HAVE YOU BEEN LISTENING TO LATELY?

A growth mindset means believing that you can get better at anything if you're willing to work hard and keep trying even when it's tough. It's not just about being naturally smart or talented. People with a growth mindset know that success isn't magic. It is actually made of about 40% ability and 60% effort. That means your hard work matters more than being "good" at something immediately. Here is the big secret: PEOPLE WHO GROW THE MOST ARE THE ONES WHO LEARN HOW TO FAIL WELL. That means they don't let failure stop them. Instead, they ask, “What can I learn from this?” They remind themselves, “I can't do this... YET.” That one word “yet” can change everything.

How do you know if you have a Growth Mindset?

Here are some signs you might already think this way:

i. You enjoy learning from people around you even if they're better at something than you are.

ii. You know that to get better at anything (sports, art, math, even video games), you need to practice and put in effort.

iii. You're not afraid to admit what you're not good at, but you're willing to work on it.

iv. You don't give up easily when something is hard, you see it as a challenge you can beat.

Carol Dweck, the psychologist who popularized this concept, discovered that people with a growth mindset tend to handle challenges better, recover from setbacks faster, and achieve more long-term success, not because they're smarter, but because they believe they can get smarter. In other words, what you believe about your brain, your ability, and your worth shapes your future.

Your Mind is Not a Mirror, It's a Muscle

A mirror reflects what's there. But a muscle? It grows with use. That's exactly what your mindset is: something you can strengthen. Here's the catch, though: muscles only grow when they're challenged. The same goes for your mind.

i. When you make a mistake, that's a workout.

ii. When you try something new, that's a stretch.

iii. When you don't give up after failing, that's growth.

Your mindset doesn't just shape your learning—it shapes your identity. If you believe you're strong & resilient, you'll act that way. If you believe you're capable, you'll try again. If you believe growth is possible, you'll stop letting fear lead. The real question, therefore, is this what are you telling yourself every day? Because those quiet inner conversations are shaping your loudest outcomes. Which one do you lean toward? Let's explore that a bit more deeply.

The Story of Two Students - Bisi and Paul.

Bisi gets a poor score on a math test. She sighs and tells herself, "I'm just not a math person." She avoids doing extra work, doesn't ask for help, and continues to struggle. That's a fixed mindset in action.

Paul also gets a poor score. But instead of shutting down, he tells himself, “Okay, I didn't do well yet. I need to figure out what I missed.” He watches tutorial videos, asks his teacher questions, and joins a study group. That's the growth mindset at work. It's not just about thinking positively, it's about understanding that ability is not fixed, and that effort is meaningful.

You Are Not Born Finished

Children naturally believe they can grow. Watch a toddler learning to walk: they fall over a hundred times, yet never say, “Maybe walking's not for me.” Somewhere along the way often during school, adolescence, or after painful life experiences, we begin to internalize limiting beliefs:

“I'm not good with people.”

“I'll never be confident.”

“It's too late to start over.”

These beliefs quietly shape our choices. But here's the truth: You are not born finished. Every human brain is capable of learning, stretching, and growing at any age.

Growth mindset is not just about school or learning. It shapes:

i. Relationships: Do you believe you can become a better listener, teammate, or friend?
ii. Emotions: Do you think you can get better at managing anger, fear, or disappointment?

iii. Talents: Do you believe creativity or leadership is something you can develop, not just something you're born with? In every case, your mindset answers the question: "Can I change?"

The Brain's Secret Power: Neuroplasticity

For decades, scientists believed that the brain was fixed after childhood. But now we know the truth: the brain can grow, change, and rewire itself. This process is called neuroplasticity. Every time you learn something new or attempt something difficult, your brain builds new connections, like strengthening muscles at the gym. That's not just hopeful thinking; it's biology. Knowing this, we must ask ourselves: Am I using the power of my brain to grow? Or am I allowing outdated beliefs to hold me back?

Real People, Real Growth

1. Kelechi, Age 9: Once shy and silent, he believed he wasn't good at making friends. But with some coaching and encouragement, he started initiating conversations. Today, he leads a peer mediation group at school.
2. Fatima, Age 17: Struggled with writing and avoided English class. She started keeping a journal and reading short stories. Two years later, she won a school-wide essay competition.

3. Mr. James, Age 58: After retiring from his job as a banker, he went back to school to study art. He now teaches painting to kids in his community center and says he's never felt more fulfilled.

Growth mindset is not a stage of life, it's a way of life.

Where Mindset Meets Purpose

You might be wondering, "Why does all this stuff about mindset even matter?" Well, here's the truth: your purpose is the special reason you're here, and the difference you're meant to make isn't something that someone just gives you. It's something you discover and build over time. The only way to uncover that purpose is by believing that you can grow, learn, and become more than you are.

Right now, you might not know what you want to be or how you'll impact the world. That's totally okay. You don't need to have it all figured out. But if you're open to learning new things, willing to try (even when it's hard), and ready to grow each day, then guess what? You're already moving in the right direction.

Step by step, little by little, brick by brick, your mindset will help you find your path and your purpose.

Reflection Questions

i. What is one thing you used to struggle with that you've now improved at?

....

....

....

....

ii. Have you ever told yourself you "just can't" do something? What if that wasn't true?

....

....

....

....

iii. Who in your life models a growth mindset? What can you learn from them?

....

....

....

....

Try This Out - The "Yet" Challenge

For the next week, every time you catch yourself saying, "I can't," add the word "YET."

1. "I don't understand this... yet."
2. "I'm not confident speaking in public... yet."
3. "I haven't found my purpose... yet."

One small word can shift your entire mindset.

CHAPTER 02

UNDERSTANDING WHO YOU ARE AND WHO YOU'RE BECOMING

"We don't find ourselves; we build ourselves one choice, one belief, one experience at a time."
You are not a finished story.
You are a story still being written.

Afolake Agunbiade

Chapter 2:

UNDERSTANDING WHO YOU ARE AND WHO YOU'RE BECOMING

Before we can fully commit to growth, we must answer a deeply personal question, "**WHO DO I BELIEVE I AM?**"

Your identity is the collection of thoughts, beliefs, memories, roles, values, and labels that you associate with yourself. It has a powerful influence on how we grow, how we love, what we pursue, how we respond to life's challenges and also how we see ourselves. You are not just one word, one mistake, one grade, or one part of your personality; you are a whole, growing, amazing person, and your identity is so much bigger than what anyone else can sum up in a few words.

You are a unique combination of your personality, passion, potential, created on purpose and for a purpose. In this chapter, we'll explore how understanding your identity is the compass that guides your purpose. When we talk about "identity," we're simply talking about the special mix of everything that makes you who you are, namely:

1. Your thoughts and feelings
2. Your dreams and fears
3. Your values (what you believe is right or important)

4. Your voice and how you express yourself
5. Your name, gender, and culture
6. Your personality traits (e.g., "I'm shy," "I'm a go-getter")
7. Your roles (student, daughter, father, sister, doctor, artist, entrepreneur)
8. Your past experiences that are good or bad.
9. Your core beliefs about your worth, potential, and purpose
10. Even how you treat others and how you see the world

Your identity acts like a filter, as it influences what you believe is possible for you. It's not cast in stone, but many of us treat it like it is. The beauty of this journey is that you get to explore, grow, and change as you learn more about yourself, and as you learn and grow through experiences, friendships, mistakes, and discoveries, you begin to shape the kind of person you're becoming.

Why This Matters

Knowing yourself helps you because when you know who you are, it's a whole lot easier to figure out what you want to do with your life and what kind of difference you want to make. So, in this chapter, we're going to ask questions, play with ideas, and give you some tools to explore your identity. The more you understand who you are now, the stronger and clearer your steps will be toward who you're becoming.

Identity; is it fixed or flexible? Have you ever heard

someone say:

i. "I'm just not creative."
ii. "I've always been the quiet one."
iii. "I'm not leadership material."
iv. "That's just the way I am."

These are not just personality descriptions. They're *identity statements* and when repeated enough, they become *identity traps*. But the real truth is that **Identity is not fixed.** You have the power to reshape your story at any time.

The Danger of Labels

From a young age, we get labelled with all sorts of things like:

i. The "smart one"
ii. The "troublemaker"
iii. The "creative one"
iv. The "slow learner"
v. The "gifted child"
vi. The "talkative"

vii. The "stubborn one"
viii. The "student."
ix. The "quiet one."
x. The "firstborn."

These labels can create pressure or limitation. If you're told you're "brilliant," you might fear failure and avoid challenges. If you're told you're "not good enough," you might stop trying altogether. I was called "The Talkative", and for many years it felt like a really bad label, but thankfully, I turned it around in university with the help of God and the growth mindset into becoming TALK-ACTIVE!

Interestingly, talk became my superpower as I now use it to teach, inspire, coach, mentor, and impact countless people, from children, preteens, teenagers, young adults, and oldies. Always remember that labels shape expectations, expectations shape identity, and identity shapes behaviour. Breaking free starts with asking, *"Is this label helping or stopping me?"* because if you believe that you are:

i. A *failure* → You may stop trying after one mistake
ii. A *learner* → You'll keep adjusting until you improve
iii. An *introvert* → You may avoid leadership or connection
iv. A *deep thinker* → You may seek out roles where your insight is valued

When your identity supports your growth, it becomes a launch pad but when your identity blocks growth, it becomes a prison. You get to choose which one it will be, so choose today.

Three Pillars of Identity - To understand who you are, reflect on these three key areas:

1. Design (How you're wired)

i. What energizes or drains you?

ii. Are you a thinker, feeler, planner, or doer?

2. Desire (What drives you)

i. What makes you excited, angry, or curious?

ii. What problems are you drawn to solve?

3. Direction (What draws you forward)

i. Where do you feel called or pulled?

ii. What values shape your decisions?

These clues point to your authentic self and your deeper purpose

The Layers of You - Identity Map

Try to identify the key influences that have shaped your self-image, how you see yourself, and what you think you're capable of.

Layer	Example, Influences
Personal	Strengths, Flaws, Dreams, Values
Family	Expectations, Roles, Labels, Stereotypes
Culture/Society	Gender roles (Girl or Boy), Religious Beliefs, Social Media
Life Experiences	Trauma, Success, Loss, and Achievements
Faith/Spirituality	Beliefs about life's meaning, your origin, your soul, your spirit

Identity and Purpose: Is there a Connection? Who You Are + What You Do = Your Purpose

Purpose is like your "why. "It's that deep feeling inside that says:

1. “I was made for something meaningful.”
2. “My life has value.”
3. “I want to make a difference in my own way.”

Purpose isn't just about what you want to do when you grow up. It's also about the kind of person you want to become.

i. Are you someone who helps others?
ii. Are you someone who creates?
iii. Do you lead?
iv Or you are someone who listens?

(You might be all of these things!) Also, sometimes, people work hard to reach goals, but they don't stop to ask themselves, “Is this the kind of person I want to be?” Because when Identity and purpose don't match, you might feel confused, lost, or like you're pretending to be someone you're not.

Ask yourself these questions:

i. What kind of person do I want to become?

ii. What do I want people to remember about me?

iii. What kind of difference do I want to make in the world?

When your identity (who you are) and your purpose (what you care about and why) start to connect, your life begins to feel more exciting, more focused, and more you. Your purpose grows best when it's planted in a strong, healthy sense of who you are and who you're becoming. And guess what? You don't have to figure it all out right now. Just keep asking good questions, learning, and growing.

Here's how identity fuels purpose:

If you believe…	Then you will…
"I am creative."	Look for ways to express ideas
"I am resilient."	Bounce back after failure
"I am a helper."	Find joy in serving others
"I am curious."	Keep learning new things
"I am unworthy."	Shrink from opportunities

Some labels are limiting. Others are lies. And even the "good" ones can become pressure traps. The problem with labels is that they put you in a box, but your purpose needs space to grow. A growth mindset says, "I am evolving. I am not defined by what I've been called because I am becoming who I was created to be." You don't just *find* your purpose; you *live into it* through what you believe about yourself.

Rewriting the Identity Story

To walk in purpose, you must challenge old stories and write a new narrative. Here is how to do so:

1. **Name the false labels.** What have you believed or have been called that doesn't serve your growth?
2. **Replace them with truth.** What does your life and even your faith say is true about you?
3. **Live into the new identity.** Let your actions reflect who you *want* to become, not who you've been told you are.

Real Stories of Identity Discovery

i. **Emma (Age 16):** Always called "the stubborn one," he later discovered he had strong convictions and leadership ability. Today, he's a student activist and speaker.

ii. **Tonye, Age 22:** Grew up hearing "be tough", "boys don't cry". He began to feel ashamed of his emotions. Through therapy, he learned that emotional expression is not weakness but wisdom. He's now studying psychology to help other young men break free.

iii. **Stella (Age 30):** Labelled "too quiet" as a child, she later embraced her deep listening and reflection skills as her superpower. She's now a sought-after therapist.

iv. **Tolu (Age 9):** Felt dumb in math until her tutor described her as a “problem solver in progress.” That mindset shift helped her improve dramatically.

Reflection Questions

i. What labels have I carried that may be holding me back?

....

....

....

....

ii. When do I feel most “myself”?

....

....

....

....

iii. Who in my life sees the real me and reminds me of my value?

....

....

....

....

iv. What labels (good or bad) have you accepted about yourself?

....

....

....

....

....

v. Are there parts of your identity that no longer serve you?

....

....

....

....

vi. What new identity do you want to grow into?

....

....

....

....

vii. What kind of person do you want to become in the next 5 years?

....

....

....

....

Growth mindset isn't just about new skills but it's also about giving yourself a new name, a new story, and a new direction.

CHAPTER 03

DON'T LET FEAR BOSS YOU AROUND

"Everything you want is on the other side of fear."

Jack Canfield

Chapter 3:

DON'T LET FEAR BOSS YOU AROUND

Have you ever wanted to try something new like trying out for a team, speaking up in class, or showing your art to someone but then that little voice in your head whispered, "What if people laugh at you?" "What if you're not good enough?" That voice is fear and it shows up for everyone.

Fear is a feeling that tries to protect you. It's like a warning bell in your brain saying, "Be careful!" That's a good thing when there's real danger like a hot stove or a speeding car. But sometimes fear shows up when there's no real danger, just the chance of being embarrassed or getting it wrong. When we listen to that fear too much, it can hold us back from growing, learning, and finding our purpose.

Imagine you're standing in front of a closed door labelled "Purpose." You reach for the handle, but something stops you. It's not locked. It's not blocked. It's just fear whispering, *"What if it's too hard?"* or *"What if you fail?"* Fear is a normal part of life. But for many of us, it becomes a powerful barrier between where we are and where we want to be. In this chapter, we're going to shine a light on fear:

i. Where it comes from

ii. What it wants, and

iii. How to grow stronger than it.

Fear is a natural emotional response to danger, real or imagined. It's your body's way of trying to protect you. It shows up when: -

i. You face something new or unfamiliar

ii. You feel out of control

iii. You imagine worst-case scenarios

iv. You believe failure or rejection is coming

But here's the problem, fear doesn't always tell the truth. It acts like an overprotective friend, trying to keep you safe, but also keeping you small.

The Different Faces of Fear

Fear doesn't always look like panic or running away. Sometimes it disguises itself subtly in:

i. Perfectionism – "I can't start until it's perfect."

ii. Procrastination – "I'll do it later when I'm ready."

iii. Comparison – "Others are better than me."

iv. Excuses – "I'm too busy," "I'm too young/old," "It's not the right time."

v. Self-doubt – "Who do I think I am to try this?"

Whether you're 13, 30, or 50, these fears are universal. But they don't have to define your path if you find the courage and strength to walk the growth mindset journey.

Fear keeps you:

i. From trying new things
ii. From asking questions
iii. From dreaming big
iv. From speaking up
v. From taking the first step

And when you avoid these things, you avoid the very experiences that lead to growth and clarity about your purpose. Fear doesn't just stop motion rather it stops YOU from becoming. A truth to remember is that courage is not the absence of fear. Courage is choosing to move forward despite the fear. You can be scared and still show up. You can feel nervous and still take action. You can fail once and still keep going. Every time you face fear, you train your brain and heart to believe - *"I can do hard things."*

Stories of Courage Over Fear

i. **Zarah, Age 12**: She used to hide at the back of class, terrified to speak. But after one small success presenting a book report, she began volunteering to lead group work. She now wants to become a teacher.

ii. **Uche, Age 35**: After losing his job, he feared starting over. With coaching and support, he built a small tech business and now trains teenagers in digital skills.

iii. **Mrs. Stella, Age 45**: After years of putting others first, she feared going back to school. But she enrolled, took one class at a time, and today, she's a certified counsellor.

The fact of the matter is that none of them were fearless. They were just brave enough to begin.

What fear is trying to teach you that you need to learn:

Instead of asking, "Why am I afraid?", try asking: "What is this fear trying to protect me from or teach me?" Here's how to decode your fear:

Fear Says...	It Might Mean...
"What if I fail?"	You care deeply about the outcome.
"What if they laugh at me?"	You're craving acceptance or confidence.
"What if I mess up?"	You need permission to grow through mistakes.
"What if I don't know how?"	You're being invited to learn something new.

When you get curious about fear, it loses its power.

The Growth Mindset Response to Fear

i. Instead of "I can't," say "I haven't mastered this yet."

ii. Instead of "What if I fail?" say "What if I succeed... or grow either way?"

iii. Instead of "I'm scared," say "I'm learning to be brave."

Please remember that fear is a signal, not a stop sign.

Try This Out - Your "Fear to Fuel" Challenge

1. Write down one thing you've been avoiding because of fear.
2. List the fear in one sentence (e.g., "I'm afraid I'll be embarrassed").
3. Ask: What's the worst that could happen?
4. Ask: What's the best that could happen?
5. Take one small action toward that thing; just one.

Do this once a week for the next month and track how you feel. You might surprise yourself.

Reflection Questions

i. What's one fear that's been holding you back?

....

....

....

....

ii. When did you last feel fear but push through anyway?

....

....

....

....

iii. Who inspires you with their courage, and why?

....

....

....

....

iv. What might your life look like if fear didn't make your decisions?

....

....

....

....

CHAPTER 04

REDEFINING FAILURE – OOPS! WHY MISTAKES HELP YOU GROW

"I have not failed. I've just found 10,000 ways that won't work."

Thomas Edison

Chapter 4:

REDEFINING FAILURE – OOPS! WHY MISTAKES HELP YOU GROW

Let's be real—no one likes to fail. It can feel frustrating, embarrassing, or even scary. But what if we told you that failure isn't the end of the road... It's part of the journey!

What if failure isn't a sign you're not good enough?
What if failure is simply feedback?
What if failure is the very thing that shapes your success?

In this chapter, we'll shift our mindset about failure from something to avoid to something to *embrace*.

What is Failure?

Failure is often defined as "not achieving a desired outcome." But let's take that further. What if failure is learning the difference between what doesn't work on the journey and what does? Failure means something didn't go the way you planned. Maybe you didn't make the team, maybe your idea didn't work, or maybe you forgot your lines at the school play.

Guess what? That's okay. Every time you "fail," you're getting a chance to grow, learn something new, and get better.

You weren't born knowing how to walk, spell your name, ride a bike, or solve problems. You fell, got back up, adjusted, and tried again. You didn't fail, you learned. Somewhere along the way, though, we began to believe that mistakes meant something was *wrong* with us. And that's the real failure: the lie that mistakes define our worth. Think of failure like a stepping stone. Each step (even the hard ones) brings you closer to your purpose.

A fixed mindset sees failure as a personal flaw, proof of being "not good enough," and a reason to stop trying, but a growth mindset sees failure as temporary, a sign of effort and an invitation to improve. If you never fail, it probably means you're not challenging yourself enough.

Real Stories, Real Setbacks

i. **Sola (Age 16)**: She didn't make the debate team on her first try. She almost gave up. But she reviewed her feedback, worked on her voice and confidence, and made the team the next year—then became captain.

ii. **Mona (Age 27)**: Started a photography business that didn't get many clients. He closed it down. But what he learned about lighting and branding helped him land a job at a media company—and now he trains other creatives.

iii. **Grandma Grace (Age 62)**: Tried baking for the first time and messed up the recipe. Instead of giving up, she laughed, tried again, and now runs a small baking business from home.

Failure didn't stop them. It just *redirected* them!

Why Failure is essential on the path to Purpose

Believe it or not, failure is actually good for you, especially when you're trying to figure out your purpose. Here are a few reasons why:

1. **Failure Makes You Tougher**
   When things don't go your way, you learn how to keep trying instead of giving up. Each time you bounce back, you're building something called resilience—that's a superpower that helps you keep going, even when stuff gets hard.

2. **Failure Helps You Find the Right Path**
   Sometimes, trying something and getting it wrong helps you figure out what's right for you. It's like taking a wrong turn, realizing it, and then finding a better route.

3. **Failure Teaches You to Take Charge**
   Instead of blaming someone else or getting mad, failure can help you stop and ask, "What could I do differently next time?" That's how real growth begins.

4. **Failure Makes You Kinder**
   When you know how it feels to mess up, you become more understanding when others do too. That's how you become a better friend, teammate, or leader—someone who doesn't laugh at others or judges them, but lifts them up.

Flip the Script - Turning Failure Forward

Let's turn some common failure beliefs into growth declarations:

Old Belief	Growth Mindset Flip
"I'm not good at this."	"I'm still learning how to do this."
"I failed, so I should stop."	"I failed, so I now know one way that doesn't work."
"Others don't fail like me."	"Everyone fails; they just don't always talk about it."
"I'm embarrassed."	"Being brave sometimes feels uncomfortable and that's okay."

Lessons Failure Teaches (That Success Can't).
Success feels good, but failure *builds you*.

i. You learn grit.
ii. You discover new strategies.
iii. You develop inner strength.
iv. You realize your worth isn't tied to outcomes.

The road to purpose is paved with wrong turns. Every misstep brings a lesson and every lesson brings you closer to clarity.

🚀 How to Bounce Back Like a Champ by Turning Mistakes into Superpowers

Messing up doesn't mean you should give up. It just means it is time to try again, and smarter this time! Here's how you can learn from mistakes and move forward like a boss.

1. **● Pause & Think, ask yourself:**

i. "What went wrong?"

ii. "What did I hope would happen?"

Thinking it through helps you understand where things changed.

2. **🙋‍♂️ Take Responsibility - Instead of blaming others, ask yourself:**

i. "What was my part in this?"

ii. "What can I do differently next time?"

Owning your part helps you grow stronger and wiser.

3. **🗣 Ask for Help - Talk to someone you trust, a parent, teacher, coach, or friend, and say:**

I. "What do you think I could do better?"

ii. Other people might see things you missed! And they do, most of the time, because, come to think of it, you are one person and your perspective may not be wholly 360 degrees!'

4. **🔄 Try Again… a Bit Differently**

i. Don't give up, switch it up! Change your plan a little and see what works better.

5. **🎉 Be Proud You Tried**

i. Even if it didn't go perfectly, you showed courage by trying. That makes you awesome already.

Try This Out - The "Failure File"

Create a "Failure File" or journal. For each failure, write:

i. What did you try?

ii. What didn't work?

iii. What you learned?

iv. What you'll try next?

Review it monthly. You'll be amazed at your growth over time.

Reflection Questions

i. What's one failure that hurt at the time but taught you something valuable?

....

....

....

....

ii. What does failure currently mean to you, and what do you want it to mean instead?

....

....

....

....

iii. How do you respond when you see others fail? Do you act graciously with them? Can you show yourself that same grace?

....

....

....

....

iv. What's one risk you're now willing to take, even if failure is possible?

....

....

....

....

CHAPTER 05

THE POWER OF RELATIONSHIPS AND SURROUNDING YOURSELF WITH GROWTH ALLIES

"You are the total average of the five people you spend the most time with."

Jim Rohn

Chapter 5:

THE POWER OF RELATIONSHIPS AND SURROUNDING YOURSELF WITH GROWTH ALLIES

Have you ever noticed how your energy changes depending on who you're with? Some people make you feel like you can do anything. Others make you doubt everything. That's because relationships are powerful as they shape how you think, feel, and grow. In this chapter, we'll explore how the people around you can either feed your growth or freeze it. And we'll learn how to build a circle that supports your journey of finding purpose.

We All Want to Belong

Whether you're a child trying to fit in at school or an adult seeking meaningful connections at work or in your community, we all crave belonging. A sense of belonging is powerful as it helps us feel safe, seen, and supported. But there's a catch, as we sometimes trade our growth for acceptance.

i. We dim our lights to fit in. I know this one, personally; I can relate.

ii. We pretend not to care, so we don't look "too ambitious."

iii. We stay silent so we don't rock the boat.

But real belonging doesn't require you to shrink, it allows you to *stretch*, grow, and thrive!

The Growth Mindset and Relationships

A growth mindset isn't just about how *you* think, it's about the environment that supports that thinking. Here's how relationships impact your mindset:

Fixed Mindset Relationships	Growth Mindset Relationships
Criticize mistakes	Help you learn from mistakes
Compete and compare	Celebrate and collaborate
Make you feel "less than"	Challenge you to be your best self
Shut down dreams	Asks, "How can I support you?"
Drain your energy	Fuel your vision

You can't grow in a place where you're constantly defending and fighting for your worth.

The 5 Types of People in Your Circle

Let's talk about the kinds of people that commonly show up in our lives and what to do with each of them:

1. **The Cheerleader** – They believe in you, even when you don't. Their support boosts your confidence.
2. **The Coach** – They give you honest feedback to help you improve. Their challenge helps you grow.
3. **The Critic** – They focus on what's wrong. You may learn from them, but too much of their voice can damage your mindset.

4. **The Companion** – They walk with you through highs and lows. Their presence reminds you that you're not alone.
5. **The Complainer** – They always focus on what's not working. Their negativity can weigh down your dreams.

Evaluate your circle with these questions:

i. Who lifts you up?

ii. Who pulls you down?

iii. Who stretches you?

iv. Who stresses you?

How to Build a Growth Circle

If your current relationships aren't growth-minded, don't worry. You can *intentionally* build a new support system. This is HOW:

1. Be the kind of person you want to attract. Growth attracts growth.
2. Seek out learning spaces like social clubs, online communities, study groups, faith groups, and professional forums.
3. Ask questions. Growth-minded people love to share what they're learning.
4. Be open to mentors. They may not be older, just more experienced in a certain area.

5. Limit toxic influences. You don't have to cut people off, but you can reduce how much of their voice you let in.

Real Stories of Growth Through Relationships

i. **Ada (Age 10):** Struggled with her math homework until a classmate invited her to join a study group. Together, they improved and became friends who encouraged each other in other subjects as well.

ii. **Caleb (Age 23):** Felt stuck after university. He found a mentor through a youth group who guided him in discovering his strengths. Today, he runs a digital design agency.

iii. **Mrs. Agnes (Age 47):** After years of playing small, she joined a women's accountability group. Weekly conversations challenged her to apply for promotions, and she eventually became regional manager. They all found people who said, *"I see you. I believe in your future."*

Protecting Your Energy While Growing

As you grow, not everyone will understand your journey. That's okay. Sometimes, growing means:

i. Spending less time with negative influences

ii. Saying "no" to gossip, drama, and comparison

iii. Setting boundaries that protect your focus

iv. Being okay with not being liked by everyone

You don't need everyone to cheer for you. You just need a few voices who tell you to "Keep going. You're becoming who you were meant to be."

Try This: The "Relationship Audit"

Take a blank sheet of paper and draw three circles:

i. **Inner Circle (Closest to you):** List 3–5 people who energize, support, or challenge you.

ii. **Middle Circle (Friends/acquaintances):** List people who influence you but aren't as close.

iii. **Outer Circle (Distant voices):** This includes social media, culture, or celebrities you follow.

Ask yourself:

i. Who belongs in my inner circle?

ii. Who needs to move further out?

iii. Who could I invite in?

Reflection Questions

i. Who in your life helps you believe in yourself?

....

....

....

....

ii. Who challenges you to grow without judging you?

....

....

....

....

iii. Are there any relationships you need to redefine or release?

....

....

....

....

iv. How can you become a better growth ally to others?

....

....

....

....

CHAPTER 06

OWNING YOUR VOICE – SPEAKING BOLDLY ABOUT WHO YOU ARE

"Don't shrink yourself to make others comfortable. Speak the truth, even if your voice shakes."

Unknown

Chapter 6:

OWNING YOUR VOICE – SPEAKING BOLDLY ABOUT WHO YOU ARE

You've spent your whole life being told who you are by parents, teachers, friends, social media, and society.

But have *you* ever truly told the world *who you are*?

Have you had something important to say but felt too shy, nervous, or unsure to speak up?

or maybe you've said something, but later wondered, "Did I say the right thing? Did I sound smart enough? Did they hear me?"

If that sounds familiar, guess what? You're not alone.

Finding and using your voice can feel scary sometimes. But here's the truth: your voice matters. And the world needs it because finding your purpose isn't just about knowing what you're good at. It's about having the boldness to speak it even when it's hard. Your voice isn't just about speaking out loud but rather about how you express yourself - your thoughts, feelings, opinions, and even your boundaries. It's about being able to say:

- "This is who I am."
- "This is what I care about."
- "This is what I need."
- "This is what I believe."

And guess what? You can do all of that boldly, without being loud, rude, or trying to impress anyone. Speaking boldly means being clear, being kind, and being you even when it feels a little uncomfortable.

Why is Owning Your Voice So Important?

When you learn to speak up with confidence:

i. People begin to understand who you truly are
ii. You build stronger friendships and relationships
iii. You're less likely to be pressured into things that don't feel right
iv. You start leading others by example
v. And most of all, you start believing in yourself

But here's the best part: owning your voice doesn't mean you have to be perfect. It just means you're learning to trust yourself and being honest about what you think, feel, and need.

You don't have to wait to be older, smarter, or more "important" to speak up. You have a voice now, and it's already powerful. So, in this chapter, we're going to explore how silence can steal your purpose, and how to speak up with courage, clarity, and kindness, no matter your age. It will also highlight:

i. How to discover what matters most to you

ii. How to speak up respectfully, even when it's hard
iii. How to say "no" when you need to
iv. How to stand up for others and what's right
v. And how to believe that your voice deserves space, always

What Does It Mean to "Own Your Voice"?

To own your voice means to:

i. Know what you believe
ii. Say what you mean
iii. Stand for what matters to you
iv. Share your story even when it's messy, and
v. Speak up when others stay silent.

Your voice is your **identity in motion**. When you use it well, it builds confidence. When you silence it, you shrink your potential.

Why Many People Stay Silent

Let's be honest, using your voice can feel scary because of these reasons:

i. **Fear of judgment** – "What if they laugh or disagree?"
ii. **Fear of rejection** – "What if I'm not accepted anymore?"
iii. **Fear of being wrong** – "What if I mess up?"
iv. **Low self-worth** – "Who am I to speak?"

But here's the truth: *Your voice matters, even if it's not perfect.*

The Growth Mindset and Your Voice

People with a growth mindset don't wait until they're perfect to speak. They understand that speaking up is part of growing up. They say:

i. "I might get this wrong, but I'm willing to try."
ii. "I have something to say, even if my voice shakes."
iii. "I'm learning to use my voice in love, not fear."

Why Your Voice is a Key to Purpose

i. Your voice expresses your values. If you don't speak up, people won't know what you stand for.
ii. Your voice attracts your tribe. People can't support you if they don't know who you are.
iii. Your voice creates impact. You may say something that helps *someone else* find their way.
iv. Your voice sets boundaries. It helps you say, "No," "I need help," or "That's not okay."

When you speak from a place of truth, you walk in purpose, even in small ways.

Real Voices, Real Boldness

i. **Zoe (Age 12):** She started a kindness club at school after noticing kids being bullied. Her voice changed the culture of her class.

ii. **Lana (Age 18):** He began a podcast about teenage mental health. His honesty helped hundreds of listeners feel seen.

iii. **Ngozi (Age 35):** After years of hiding her art, she began sharing her poems online. Now, her words inspire others to embrace healing.

You don't have to be famous to make a difference. You just have to be *faithful* to your voice.

How to Find and Use Your Voice

1. **Know what matters to you** - What makes you excited, angry, or passionate? That's a clue.
2. **Practice self-expression** - Start a journal, vlog, blog, or voice note. Speak your thoughts out loud, even just to yourself.
3. **Speak with humility, not fear** - It's okay not to have all the answers. Just share what you *do* know with kindness.
4. **Set boundaries** - You're allowed to say, "I don't like that," or "That's not who I am." That's owning your truth.
5. **Stand up for others** - Sometimes your voice is needed to protect someone else's dignity.

Try This Out - "I Am, I Value, I Speak" Exercise

Write three sentences:

i. **I am:** Describe who you are in one bold sentence. ("I am a creative thinker who sees beauty in broken things.")

ii. **I value:** Share one core belief. ("I value honesty because it sets people free.")

iii. **I speak:** Declare how you will use your voice. ("I speak to help others believe in themselves.")

Put it on your wall, screen, or notebook. Read it often.

Reflection Questions

i. What are 3 things you wish more people knew about you?

....

....

....

....

ii. What's something you believe in so deeply that you would speak up for it, even if it was unpopular?

....

....

....

....

iii. When was the last time you stayed silent but wished you had spoken up?

....

....

....

....

iv. How can you start using your voice more—at home, at school, at work, online?

....

....

....

....

CHAPTER 07

FROM DREAMING TO DOING – HOW TO SET GROWTH GOALS THAT MATTER

"A goal without a plan is just a wish."

Antoine de Saint-Exupéry

Chapter 7:

FROM DREAMING TO DOING – HOW TO SET GROWTH GOALS THAT MATTER

You've explored your mindset, embraced your identity, and discovered hints of your purpose. Now comes the part that scares many people: actually turning those dreams into action. It's one thing to dream. It's another thing entirely to *do*. In this chapter, we'll break down how to set meaningful goals that grow with you, and not pressure you. You'll learn to create a rhythm of action that is honest, healthy, and aligned with your purpose.

Why Most People Avoid Goal Setting

Let's face it: the idea of goal-setting can feel overwhelming. Why?

i. Fear of failure ("What if I don't achieve it?")

ii. Perfectionism ("It has to be the perfect goal.")

iii. Past disappointments ("I've tried before and quit.")

iv. Distraction ("Life gets busy and I lose focus.")

v. Comparison ("My goals seem smaller than others'.")

But the fact is that - growth isn't about setting the biggest goals. It's about staying faithful to the right ones.

The Growth Mindset Approach to Goals

A growth mindset changes how we set goals. Instead of asking "How do I win or prove myself?" We ask: "How can I grow and stay consistent?"

People with a growth mindset:

i. Focus on **progress**, not **perfection**
ii. Break big dreams into small steps
iii. Learn from mistakes and setbacks
iv. Celebrate effort, not just outcomes

The 4 "E" Framework for Growth Goals - Use these four steps to move from *dreaming* to *doing*.

1. **Explore – What do I want to grow in?** Ask yourself:

i. What excites me right now?
ii. Where do I feel I need to stretch?
iii. What have I been avoiding but want to overcome?

Example: "I want to grow in speaking up at school." "I want to read more books about confidence."

2. **Envision – What does success look like?** Get specific. Paint a picture of what growth might look like.

i. "By the end of this term, I want to have shared at least one idea in every group project."
ii. "I want to finish 4 personal growth books this year."

3. **Execute – What small steps can I take today?** Break the goal down into small, achievable steps.

i. "Write down 3 topics I care about."
ii. "Practice sharing one opinion at dinner."
iii. "Schedule 10 minutes of reading every day."

4. **Evaluate – What's working, what's not?** Check in with yourself.

i. Am I making progress?
ii. Do I need to adjust the goal?
iii. What have I learned about myself?

This rhythm builds not just discipline but self-trust.

SMART Goals with a Purpose Twist

Let's look at how to make your goals SMART, but with purpose-driven lens:

Smart	Purpose-Twist Question
Specific	Is this goal connected to something meaningful to me?
Measurable	How will I know I'm growing, even in small ways?
Achievable	Does this stretch me without stressing me
Relevant	Does this align with my values and identity?
Time-bound	When will I check in on my progress, not just results?

Stories of Growth in Action

i. Isioma (Age 10): Struggled with shyness. Her goal? Raise her hand at least once a week in class. She began to grow into a leader among her peers.

ii. Aliyu (Age 22): Felt stuck in self-doubt. His goal? Read one personal growth book each month. His mindset transformed within a year.

iii. Mrs. Grace (Age 47): Wanted to improve connection with her teenage daughter. She set a goal to have “no-phone” chats twice a week. Their relationship deepened.

Small steps eventually bring big changes.

Reflection Questions

i. What's one area in your life you want to grow right now?

....

....

....

....

ii. What's one small goal you can set today that aligns with your purpose?

....

....

....

....

iii. How will you stay kind to yourself if things don't go perfectly?

....

....

....

....

....

iv. Who can help support and encourage you as you grow?

....

....

....

....

CHAPTER 08

NAVIGATING SETBACKS – HOW TO STAY ON TRACK WHEN LIFE GETS MESSY

"Fall seven times, stand up eight."

Japanese Proverb

Chapter 8:

NAVIGATING SETBACKS – HOW TO STAY ON TRACK WHEN LIFE GETS MESSY

Let's be honest with the fact that life doesn't always go the way we expect.

Sometimes we study hard for a test and still don't get the grade we wanted. Sometimes friendships get complicated and leave us feeling confused or hurt. Sometimes we try something new like joining a team, performing on stage, or sharing our idea and it just doesn't work out. These moments are called setbacks. They're the bumps in the road that slow us down, shake our confidence, or make us wonder if we're even heading in the right direction.

Guess what? Everyone faces setbacks. Even the most successful, talented, or confident people you admire have been through hard or messy moments. What makes them strong isn't that they never fail;, rather it's that they learn how to keep going.

What is a setback, really?

A setback is anything that makes you feel stuck, discouraged, or off-track from what you hoped would happen. It could be:

i. Getting left out or feeling misunderstood
ii. Losing something you cared about
iii. Making a big mistake
iv. Feeling overwhelmed or unsure of what to do next
v. A bad grade after weeks of study
vi. A relapse into old habits
vii. Getting rejected for an opportunity
viii. Losing motivation halfway through your goal

But here's the secret:

i. Setbacks aren't stop signs.
ii. They're learning moments.
iii. They help you build strength, courage, patience, and problem-solving skills.

They give you the chance to press pause, reflect, try again with more wisdom than before with an invitation to grow stronger, smarter, and more grounded. This chapter is here to remind you that it's okay to mess up, get stuck, or feel like quitting sometimes. It also is here to show you how to bounce back. You'll learn:

i. How to talk to yourself kindly when things don't go right
ii. What to do when you feel like giving up
iii. How to spot lessons in your disappointments

iv. Why setbacks can actually help you grow into your purpose

v. And how to keep moving forward even if it's one small step at a time

So, if things feel messy right now or if you're just trying to be ready for the next challenge, this chapter is your guide. Let's build the skills to stay steady and strong, no matter what life throws your way. Setbacks aren't failures, they're feedback.

The Mindset Shift: From Failure to Feedback

People with a fixed mindset believe:

i. "If I mess up, it means I'm not good enough."

ii. "If I fall behind, I might as well quit."

People with a growth mindset believe:

i. "Every fall is a chance to stand taller."

ii. "Setbacks don't cancel my purpose, they refine it."

You're not starting from scratch; you're starting with better insight from your experiences.

Four (4) Truths About Setbacks

1. **Everyone has them -** Even the most successful people have stumbled, doubted themselves, and had to start over.

2. **They don't define you -** You are not your worst moment. You are what you choose to learn from it.
3. **They reveal what needs work -** A setback shows where you need support, new strategies, or better boundaries.
4. **They can become setups for growth -** The lesson inside your setback may be the exact key you need for your next breakthrough.

Common Setbacks and How to Respond

Setback	Growth Response
Procrastination	Break the task into tiny, doable steps. Start with 5 minutes.
Discouragement	Revisit your "why." Talk to someone who believes in you. (Book a session with me)
Distractions	Eliminate or reduce triggers. Schedule focused time blocks.
Failure	Ask: "What can I learn from this? What would I do differently?"
Burnout	Rest. Refocus. Restore. Growth is not hustle, it's healthy consistency.

Emotional First Aid for Setbacks:

1. **Pause and Breathe** - Don't panic. Take 3 deep breaths and acknowledge what you're feeling.
2. **Name the Setback Honestly** - Say what happened without shame. Example: "I missed my reading goal for the week."
3. **Respond with Compassion, Not Criticism** - Talk to yourself the way you'd talk to a friend "This is tough, but it doesn't mean I'm a failure." "I've bounced back before; I can do it again."
4. **Get Back in Motion** - What's one small action you can take today to move forward?

Real-Life Recovery Stories

i. **Olu (Age 14):** Was building a blog and quit after no one read her first post. She restarted, wrote from her heart, and now gets hundreds of views per week.

ii. **Ahmed (Age 19):** Failed his first driving test and almost gave up. After practicing and reflecting on his nerves, he passed the second time with confidence.

iii. **Mrs. Enitan (Age 45):** Started a business and lost money early. Instead of quitting, she found a mentor, learned financial literacy, and built a thriving brand.

Setback Recovery Plan

Whenever you face a setback, journal your answers to these:

1. What happened? (Describe it honestly)
2. What emotions am I feeling right now?
3. What might this setback be teaching me?
4. What can I do differently next time?
5. What's that one step I can take to keep going?
6. What setback has shaken your confidence recently?
7. What would it look like to be kind to yourself in this moment?
8. Who can you talk to, without judgement, about your journey?

CHAPTER 09

THE POWER OF COMMUNITY AND WHY YOU NEED SUPPORT TO GROW

> "If you want to go fast, go alone. If you want to go far, go together."
>
> African Proverb

Chapter 9:

THE POWER OF COMMUNITY AND WHY YOU NEED SUPPORT TO GROW

Have you ever tried to carry something heavy all by yourself? It's tough, right? Now imagine someone coming along to help you lift it. Suddenly, it's easier and you can go farther, faster. That's what community does. It helps carry the weight of life because you weren't meant to grow, dream, and discover your purpose all alone. Even the strongest trees need good soil and sunlight. You need people, and people need you. We live in a world that celebrates independence, but we were created for interdependence.

Even superheroes need a team:

i. Iron Man had the Avengers.

ii. Harry Potter had Hermione and Ron.

iii. Jesus had 12 disciples.

iv. Steve Jobs had Steve Wozniak and a creative team to help build Apple.

v. Serena Williams had her sister Venus, her parents, and her coaches to support her journey.

People with a growth mindset don't just believe they can grow. They believe others can grow, too, and they help each other rise.

What Exactly Is Community?

Community isn't just a group of people standing in the same room. It's the circle of support around you, the friends, family, teachers, teammates, mentors, and even kind strangers who help you feel seen, safe, and strong.

Think of community like a garden; here's what a healthy community provides:

i. People who remind you of your strengths when you forget.

ii. Friends who challenge you to keep the promises you made to yourself.

iii. Mentors who've walked ahead and can guide your journey.

iv. A tribe that claps for you when you win and lifts you when you lose.

v. A safe place where you don't have to be perfect to be loved. You are part of someone else's garden too.

That means you also have something to give; kindness, honesty, fun, or just being a good listener.

Why Is Community So Important for Growth?

You grow faster and healthier when you're surrounded by people who:

i. Believe in you especially when you don't believe in yourself.

ii. Challenge you to be your best (and call you out when you're off-track).

iii. Celebrate your wins, even the small ones.

iv. Stick around when life gets hard.

v. Help you discover your purpose by reminding you of your gifts.

You don't need a huge community. What you need is just a few people who are honest, caring, and willing to grow with you. But, you may ask "What If I Don't Feel Like I Have a Support System?" You're not alone in that feeling. Some people have strong support at home, while others find it in clubs, youth groups, online spaces, or even books and mentors they look up to.

This chapter will help you:

i. Understand what healthy support looks like.

ii. Notice the kind of people who lift you up (and the ones who don't).

iii. Learn how to be a good friend and community member.

iv. Build strong relationships that help you grow with purpose.

v. Speak up when you need help and learn that asking for support is a strength, not a weakness because you were never meant to do life alone.

Growth takes teamwork and Purpose grows best in good company. Let's learn how to find your people, build your circle, and become the kind of person others are lucky to have in their lives.

Who Should Be in Your Growth Circle? Let's break down the kinds of people that help you grow:

1. The Encourager

i. They speak life into you. They remind you of who you are.

ii. "You've got this." "Don't give up." "I believe in you."

2. The Challenger

i. They ask the hard questions. They push you past excuses.

ii. "Why did you stop writing?" "Are you really using your time well?"

3. The Mentor

i. They've walked the road ahead and offer wisdom and direction.

ii. "Here's what I've learned…" "Let me show you another way."

4. **The Peer**

i. They're on the same journey as you. You grow together, laugh together, and share wins and wounds.

ii. "I'm working on that too!" "Let's practice together."

5. **The Safe Space**

i. This person listens without judging. You can be real with them.

ii. "You're not alone." "Thank you for being honest with me."

Building a Growth Community: How to Start

i. Look Around - Who already supports or inspires you, even in small ways?

ii. Reach Out - Send a message. Start a conversation. Say: "I'm trying to grow in……….. Would you be open to supporting me or holding me accountable?"

iii. Be Vulnerable - Let people into your struggles not just your success stories.

iv. Give What You Hope to Receive- Be an encourager. Be a good friend. Celebrate others.

v. Set Healthy Boundaries - Not everyone deserves full access. Choose wisely. Protect your peace.

What if I Feel Alone?

That's real. Sometimes we don't feel like we have anyone we can lean on. Here's what to do:

i. **Pray for your circle** – Ask God to bring the right people.

ii. **Join a community** – A youth group, book club, online learning circle e.g. The Girls Hub, or a good support group.

iii. **Be the kind of friend you need** – You'll attract your tribe in time.

Even if you feel alone now, you won't always be. Stay open to stay growing.

Reflection Questions

i. Who are the people in your life right now who help you grow?

....

....

....

....

ii. What kind of support do you need more of?

....

....

....

....

....

iii. How can you be a better part of someone else's growth journey?

....

....

....

....

iv. What small step can you take today to build deeper connection?

....

....

....

....

CHAPTER 10

BECOMING A PURPOSE-DRIVEN LEADER – INSPIRING OTHERS THROUGH YOUR GROWTH

"Leadership is not about a title or a position.
It is about impact, influence, and inspiration."

Robin Sharma

Chapter 10:

BECOMING A PURPOSE-DRIVEN LEADER – INSPIRING OTHERS THROUGH YOUR GROWTH

You've been learning how to grow, how to build resilience, cultivate the right mindset, and surround yourself with the right people. Now, let's talk about something powerful, not the kind that comes with a fancy title or corner office. We're talking about purpose-driven leadership, the kind that flows from who you are and how you live because once you start growing on the inside, you'll begin to inspire change on the outside.

What Is Purpose-Driven Leadership?

It is leadership that is rooted in:

i. Clarity of purpose – You know what you stand for.

ii. Consistency of action – You live what you believe.

iii. Compassion for others – You lift others as you rise.

Purpose driven leaders don't just seek success, they seek to make a difference. Leadership is not about being loud or bossy. It's about influence and we all influence someone.

i. The younger sibling who watches how you react to stress.

ii. The classmate who listens when you speak with confidence.

iii. The friend who follows your courage to try something new.

iv. The stranger inspired by your story.

You are leading every day by how you live, love, learn, and lead yourself.

Signs You're Becoming a Purpose-Driven Leader

1. You take responsibility for your choices.
2. You model the values you talk about.
3. You encourage growth in others, not just yourself.
4. You ask good questions before offering quick answers.
5. You're willing to go first, even when it's uncomfortable.

Growth Stage	Leadership Shift
Learning to believe in yourself	Helping others believe in themselves
Bouncing back from failure	Showing others how to stand up after falling
Building new habits	Guiding others to do the same
Finding your purpose	Creating space for others to explore theirs

You grow for you but you lead for others.

Three Roles of a Purpose-Driven Leader

1. The Example - You live your values out loud.

i. "I don't just talk about kindness, I show it."

ii. "I handle pressure with calm, and others learn from that."

2. The Encourager - You help others see their own potential.

i. "You've got a gift; don't hide it."

ii. "Keep going, even if it's hard. I believe in you."

3. The Guide-You offer wisdom, resources, or support based on your experience.

i. "Here's what helped me when I was in your shoes."

ii. "I've made mistakes too; let's learn from them together."

Leading with Humility

Leadership isn't about being perfect, but more about showing up with:

i. Integrity – Doing the right thing even when no one is watching

ii. Empathy – Understanding how others feel without judging them

iii. Courage – Making hard choices for the right reasons

Great leaders are not always the loudest, they are the most consistent.

Reflection Questions:

i. Who has inspired you through the way they live and lead?

....

....

....

....

ii. What kind of leader do you want to be remembered as?

....

....

....

....

iii. What message does your life send to the people watching you?

....

....

....

....

iv. Where can you start leading with purpose today?

....

....

....

....

CHAPTER 11

LIVING A LEGACY – HOW TO KEEP GROWING AND HELP OTHERS DO THE SAME

"Carve your name on hearts, not tombstones. A legacy is etched into the minds of others and the stories they share about you."

Shannon L. Alder

Chapter 11:

LIVING A LEGACY – HOW TO KEEP GROWING AND HELP OTHERS DO THE SAME

You've slowly taken a journey through the pages of this book on mind-sets, resilience, purpose, and leadership; here is the truth: this isn't the end. It is the beginning of your legacy because real growth doesn't stop when you feel better, do better, or know better. Real growth continues *through your habits, through your actions, and through your impact on others.* Let's explore how to live a legacy.

What Is a Legacy?

A legacy isn't just what you leave *after* you time here on earth is done. It's the life you're building right now, one thought, one word, one decision at a time. Your legacy is:

i. The way people feel after talking to you.

ii. The change you spark in your family, school, or community.

iii. The dreams you make possible because you chose to keep growing.

Your legacy is not in what you do, but in who you become and who you help others become.

Why Your Legacy Matters

1. It Gives Meaning to Your Growth - You are not growing just for yourself. You growing to *give*.
2. It Multiplies Impact - When you help one person rise, they help another. It becomes a ripple effect.
3. It Anchors Your Purpose - Living with legacy in mind keeps your values front and center.

The Legacy of a Growth Mindset

People with a growth mindset leave legacies that include:

i. Curiosity over certainty

ii. Hope over fear

iii. Resilience over giving up

iv. Possibility over limitation

v. "She kept trying, even when it was hard."

vi. "He believed in me when I didn't believe in myself."

vii. "They lived on purpose and it changed my life"

You don't need to be rich, famous, or old to build a legacy. You just need to show up with:

i. Intentional words (like "I see you." "I forgive you." "You matter.")

ii. Consistent actions (doing what you say and being who you claim to be.), and

iii. Purposeful service (Helping others grow, dream, heal, or learn.)

Legacy is built in the quiet choices nobody sees but everyone feels.

How to Keep Growing and Giving

1. Keep Learning - Never stop feeding your mind and spirit. Read. Reflect. Try new things.
2. Mentor Someone - Take what you've learned and pass it on. Be the person you once needed.
3. Live with Intention - Wake up and ask: *How can I show up with purpose today?*
4. Reflect Regularly - Check in with your values, goals, and growth. Journaling helps.
5. Celebrate Progress, Not Perfection - Your growth journey won't be flawless, but it will be *fruitful* if you stay committed.

The Legacy Letter

Write a letter to your future self or your future children/grandchildren. Start the letter with:

This is the kind of life I want to live…
These are the lessons I've learned…
This is the kind of person I'm becoming…
This is what I hope you remember me for…

Tuck it away. Come back to it. Keep becoming the person that letter describes.

Final Reflection Questions:

i. What do you want people to remember about you?

....

....

....

....

ii. How are you already building your legacy today?

....

....

....

....

iii. What message is your life sending to the world?

....

....

....

....

iv. If today were the first page of a new chapter, how would you write it?

....

....

....

....

CHAPTER 12

YOU ARE NOT STUCK; YOU ARE LEVELLING UP - THE STORY OF ZINA

Chapter 12:

YOU ARE NOT STUCK; YOU ARE LEVELLING UP - THE STORY OF ZINA

Zina was 14, just like you. She loved sketching in the margins of her school notebooks and daydreaming about being "someone big" one day. But most of the time, Zina didn't feel very big. In fact, she felt small.

i. She tried out for the school play and forgot her lines.

ii. She entered a spelling competition and was out in the first round.

iii. She joined a coding club but nothing she tried seemed to work.

Each time something didn't go as planned, Zina heard a little voice in her head whisper: "Maybe you're just not good enough." "You're not like the others." "You'll always mess up." One day, she came home after a tough school day and slumped on the couch. Her uncle noticed and handed her something unexpected: a blank comic book. On the first page, he had written:

"*Write your own origin story. Heroes aren't born perfect. They become.*"

That night, Zina began to draw her superhero: clumsy, awkward, and full of mistakes but brave enough to keep trying. Every failure gave her new powers. Every challenge made her stronger. And guess what? Somewhere between the drawings and the daydream, Zina realized something. She wasn't just creating a superhero; she was actually becoming one.

You may not feel like you're getting everything right and that's okay. That's part of the journey. Just like Zina, your *power* is not in being perfect. It's in showing up, trying again, and refusing to give up. You don't need to have it all figured out to begin your story. You just need to begin. Your growth mindset is the starting point. Your purpose is the compass. Your voice is the pen. And your identity? It's still unfolding with every choice, every step, every lesson.

Congratulations! You've made it to the final chapter, not just of this book, but of one version of your life.
Here's what Zina, and now *you,* are learning on this journey:

1. **Mindset Shapes Everything -** Your thoughts can either block your path or build a bridge to where you want to go. Growth mindset means you believe you *can* grow even when things are hard.

2. **Identity Is Not Fixed-** Who you are is not a label or one moment. It's a journey of becoming. You are always growing, evolving, discovering.

3. **Purpose Is Built, Not Found -** Purpose is not just "a job" or "a big dream." It's how you use your life to bring meaning to others and yourself. Every step, every skill, every lesson adds up.

4. **Failure Is a Superpower in Disguise -** It teaches you, stretches you, and prepares you for greater things. Don't run from it. Learn from it.

5. **Community Makes You Stronger -** You don't have to do this alone. Your "Avengers team" could be parents, friends, mentors, or even characters in books. Find your people.

Final Journal Prompt: Write a letter from your future self (five years from now) to your current self. In the letter, include:

i. What your future self is proud of

ii. What challenges you've overcome

iii. What habits helped you grow

iv. What dreams you're starting to live

If you've read this far, I want you to know something: You are not stuck. You're growing, changing, and becoming. You're in training. Every hard day, every big decision, every time you try again it all counts. You are the author of your story. You are the hero of your journey, so don't stop here. Level up because the world needs the version of you that you are still becoming and I can't wait to see what you'll do next.

A Note from the Author

You are not too young.
You are not too late.
You are not too broken.
You are *becoming*!

This book was never about being perfect, it was about planting seeds of growth, purpose, and truth inside you and now that those seeds are planted, it's time to live them out.

Remember:

You were made for more.
You have a reason for being here.
And your life, *your growth* can inspire generations to come.

Don't just live. Live on purpose.
Don't just succeed. Leave a *legacy*.